Lecron Bradley

Raising Cans

Raising the next generation of AmeriCANS

TABLE OF CONTENTS

EDUCATION

EDUCATION AND MORALS

EDUCATION: PRIVATE, PUBLIC, and

RELIGIOUS

YOUTH: Youth Then and Now

PROTECTING YOUTH

FREEDOM

PROTECTING FREEDOM

POLITICAL VIEWPOINTS

BORDER

PRO-LIFE

LGTBQ RIGHTS

STATES RIGHTS

WELFARE

BORDER CONTROL

THE SECOND AMENDMENT

GOD and COUNTRY

FREEDOM: GOD'S GIFT

SOCIAL MEDIA

REPAIRING EDUCATION

REPAIRING the YOUTH

LOOKING TOWARD the FUTURE

MATURITY

COMMUNISM, SOCIALISM, and CAPITALISM

SOLUTIONS

CLOSING

The task of raising my girls is one of the greatest honors and privileges I may ever receive. God has given me two amazing miracles, and I plan to raise them in the right, just, and moral way. I will do my best not to squander this opportunity in which I believe the prior generation has already.

This book will lay down my plan to correct societal areas, whereas I believe we have failed. We failed not only ourselves, our country, and most importantly, our children. The words in this book may be offensive to some, but this is how I see it and is only my opinion. Our children are grown-up babies with no vision or the ability to accept defeat. This has become abundantly clear with the defeat of Hillary Clinton in the last election, which has prompted me to write this book and to get my thoughts out there in the hope of real change.

I will touch on such subjects as education, religion, healthcare, and the role in which the government plays in each. I will also touch on the political right and the political left as it pertains to our youth and their views on the country. I will also touch on the constitution and our founding fathers to mesh the document's spirituality and divinity. Raising Cans is an attempt to establish common sense and critical thinking back into logical everyday thought. I would also like to touch on freedom, freedom now, and freedom in the future.

One thing is exact this nation under God will undoubtedly stand the test of time. I believe we have lost perfectionism, greatness, and exceptionalism, and we need to strive to get those back by opening our hearts and minds and seeing what has happened to these qualities and begin changing the issues. We as a nation could or as I should say, should do much better and should settle for nothing short of greatness in the pursuit of the American promise. I hope reading through the pages of this book; I can open your eyes to my opinions and ideas.

Dedicated to my girls: My wife Stacie and daughters Sophia Rose LeCron and Estella Rose LeCron.

EDUCATION

Do you ever ask yourself why the government has so much control over what we learn? I do not believe that there should be any government involvement in any institution of academics. I think that we can do a more outstanding job of educating ourselves in the private sector. Suppose they can control what and how much of the particular substance we are learning. In that case, it becomes much easier to control and manipulate the subject matter and manipulate us in return. That plays right into what I believe the leftists want for us. Total Control!

Take, for instance, our history, and if you can control someone or a group of someone's past, then you may certainly be able to dictate that someone's future. Pretty scary when you think about it in those terms. Ponder this. Can you imagine a world without its past? Or possibly that past has been rewritten to fit a particular agenda? Imagine if you will find slavery or the revolutionary war was gone removed from history. Maybe it was added to accommodate the agenda! Just think how different this nation would be.

No slavery?! We are a few generations away from the most considerable blemish in our country's history to never have even existed. All to possibly save people's feelings, to hide them from the truth, and protect them. The unfortunate part about it all is that if we do not learn from history, it will repeat itself. Possible against the same race or perhaps a different race of individuals. I wish this would not be the case, but it certainly has been proven over and over again throughout history.

Being a man of faith, I choose to believe mankind is better than these types of deplorable actions. I believe humanity is inherently good and tries to be on the right side of history. On the other hand, I think it is essential to understand that people will have tried brainwashing and mass control concepts throughout history. So, I like to pay close attention to what my children are bringing home from school. Watch closely, pay attention, and make proper adjustments as needed to keep the truth known. It is imperative not to lose sight of the truth. I know that my wife and I will do the best to educate our daughters and teach them history regardless of how ugly the truth might be. At times even unimaginable atrocities. It is hard to believe that humans can do such atrocities to one another, but it is essential to know and never forget. Moreover, we depend on our educators to, in a sense, raise our children. In fact, we pay a hefty price tag to have the partial truth be taught to protect some, which then becomes detrimental to society's fabric.

As we see in real-time, the destruction that the youth's ignorance of the truth combined with the manipulation by the leftist has caused real and lasting damage to this nation. Furthermore, if education's trajectory does not slow down, we are in for a real damaging ride to the present atmosphere and real generational ineptness. Education can change the course we are on, but the damage is deeply rooted and will take a deep and lasting commitment to regain what is stolen. I am afraid the American attitude is that the nation is too far gone, and it's easier to go with the flow in a matter of speaking. Academia in this nation must be changed and changed NOW! Academic truth will bring us closer to our nation's promise to each of us White, Black, Brown, Native, or Transplant. It doesn't fit the leftist agenda to have us, the citizens, solid and united. United we stand and united the leftist fall.

EDUCATION AND MORALS

How did we get so far away from morals? How is it we are not teaching basic moral compass to our children anymore? Understanding that at the core of an impregnable modern society is a basic moral compass is fundamental in maintaining a modern society. Morals such as respect for yourself and others, honesty, loyalty, generosity, and responsibility for personal actions are the foundation of society. It saddens me to see this moral compass dissipate at such a rapid pace; it is pretty frightening.

All the fundamentals concerning morals should start at home and flow directly into the classroom, with the same standards. As we, unfortunately, see, this is not always the case. Many parents are not upholding their end of the bargain. A teacher should not have to parent as well as educate your child. Let us take a closer look at a few of the basic morals you should bestow upon your children.

Respect for themselves and others is a significant moral that my wife and I try to work on day in and day out. It is a moral which is underestimated and undervalued these days. Respect is crucial in the development of a well-rounded youth. Manner words, for example, are straightforward: please, thank you, yes ma'am, and no sir, etc. what I do is point out when they fail to use the words, every time without fail, and you can watch the changes that begin to happen. Changes in the way your kids are viewed but also the way they view themselves. Significant adjustments happen in their lives when we drive home the fundamentals at home and hold our children accountable at school as well. Again, accountability for their actions at home and at school.

For instance, generosity is a fantastic moral to bestow on your child, particularly at an early age. We should start this ethical gift as early as possible. The giving of oneself or goods is a great way to develop a well-rounded moral compass, realizing that giving yourself both monetarily and volunteering opens a unique perspective of the world. Giving this gift to our children not only frees their souls but also opens their hearts. What a great gift is generosity to bestow on our kids. Again, it starts at home, and you should lead by example. Imagine a world with more giving, whether through charitable donations or volunteering your time; what a great gift that would be to society. My girls certainly notice the small things my wife and I do in regard to generosity. It is apparent when they bring up when we should help someone who is less fortunate. It warms my heart and affirms that my wife and I are on the right path.

Honesty with yourself and others are both equally important. Honesty is critical to the foundation of the person and his or her moral compass. I have always been an honest person, so it is hard to talk about being dishonest, but undoubtedly corrupt people exist, and it tears at the fabric of the person and society. It indeed tears at the fabric of the person and society as a whole. No one likes a dishonest person, not even the person himself or herself. Start at home and be the example. Also, continue honesty in the classroom as well.

To Raise Cans: we must bestow our children with the great gift of having morals and a well-rounded moral compass. Then we must continue the development of moral character into our educational system. It is imperative and non-negotiable that we do this in every school in every city until we bring our moral compass back to the forefront of our youth. Finally, we must demand attention from ourselves and the governing bodies of local, state, and federal municipalities.

What is profoundly disturbing is the complete lack of concern of bringing morals back to the front lines as one of the most critical issues we must face. To undo the atmosphere, the leftist has also created to not hurt others feelings, we must start with the idea of morals and the importance of a well-rounded moral compass. If we allow our youth's moral compass to continue to decay, we will become a generation away from age with a complete lack of moral compass. How scary is that? Not a place I would like to live or raise a family. Luckily, there is still time to turn the tables and get back on the right path—a path of moral enlightenment.

My wife and I are doing our part with our children, and I believe most parents are doing their best as well. Now I think the problem is and will continue to be in the educational system until we begin to raise the next generation of Cans. We must demand that morals become first in our schools at the local, state, and federal levels and hold them to bringing morals back to the main priority. It takes work at home as well, which we have failed in doing. We simply find it okay for our kids to sit in front of a tablet or smartphone and learn who knows what. We forgot what it is like to be hands-on and teach our kids morals and proper behavior. Not only should we teach our children, but we should also lead by example.

EDUCATION: PRIVATE, PUBLIC and RELIGIOUS

Let us talk about education, the pros, and the cons in the different academic areas.

Religious education, for me, was the best experience. It helped mold and shape me into the man that I am today. All the right ingredients are available to help you excel in life and, if used wisely, a fantastic tool to catapult your future to success. I was truly fortunate and had the opportunity to spend grade school and high school in these academic areas thanks to my parents' sacrifices for myself, my brother, and my sister. As a parent myself with two daughters in a religious institution, one can understand those sacrifices.

Sometimes I do wish I had continued my education. I often wonder what would I have become? In the big picture of things, I do not believe it truly matters. I have absorbed the fundamentals needed to be a successful adult with my grade school and high school education. Now with that said, if your career path requires some specialized attention, then, by all means, continue your education until your goals are realized and achieved. I know that a religious grounded institution worked for me. It certainly has given me the skills necessary to become a successful, morally entrenched adult. Removing my bias, the morals alone that are taught in the most simplistic ways find their way home in your children; what a great gift and, in my opinion, worth the sacrifice my wife and I endure.

One of the significant issues of religious education is, of course, the cost. But if we take the considerable aspects of the religious institutions and implement them into the public school system, we will do our children and society an excellent service. Invoking such things as morals, manners, and discipline, all free, free in the sense of cost, will become a fight with some leftists; however, it is for the benefit of our children and, in return, future society. We need to get the government regulations and political correctness out of the way. Get back to the basics on what made our country and citizens great!

Private academies are the same as religious academies. The same hefty price tag emphasizes manners, morals, and discipline but without religious overtones. As far as academics in private/religious education, I know schools ahead of the public school system and some schools that simply keep pace with the public schools. I know from my experience the private and religious schools are the right choice for my family.

Privatized or religious academic institutions are not an option for everyone because of the hefty price tag. Some are forced into a system of education that is not ideal for learning. Both the social and academics are in disarray in some of these environments. So, what do you do for those that genuinely want to learn? That wants a better life! Let us look at a few options: should we hold teachers accountable? Absolutely! Do we need to keep the parents accountable? Absolutely! Do we need to keep the students accountable? Again, absolutely! Our educational system is a joke, and it has failed our kids, which, in return, fails society. So, there is no viable option for success without the hefty price tag of a private school. I find this unacceptable, but who is to blame? Government! That is right.

There are roughly 50 million students that attend 98,000 public schools and 28,000 private schools nationally. The taxpayers are on the hook to ensure they get an excellent education, and we must not fail them. Greatness, perfectionism, and leadership start with our kids at home and flow in the educational system. Holding our kids, teachers, and especially ourselves accountable is critical and is the responsible thing to do. Let us be the change required to reform our broken school system and move this nation into the future. Successfully!

So, to recap, remove government regulation and intrusive idealistic agendas and replace them with learning environments. Allow the kids to use their minds to determine their ideals. Morals, morals, and morals are not too tricky if you demand this from the very beginning. If kids do not respect themselves, they certainly will not respect others. Worst they will grow up with no self-worth, and in return, their life will suffer because of their lack of self-worth. Finally, take the things that work in the private and religious institutions free and then integrate them into the public system. Let us give our kids a fighting chance to become successful! It is very hurtful to know that most of our youth are graduating from high school well below par and never truly achieving their full potential every day. We must stop allowing the child to waste their potential and start teaching them their worth and worth fighting for. The next generation of Cans can be and should be the greatest generation we produce if we arm them with the correct information, starting with public schools. We all pay a tremendous amount of money in taxes to not demand the best from our government, public schools, and teachers. Our kids are indeed worth that much.

Now not all public institutions are deplorable, but certainly, the ones in our inner cities and large cities across the nation are, and this is where we educate our youths. It is time to take a hard look at what is working and what is not and change the things that are not as soon as possible. There are plenty of great teachers out there that are extraordinarily successful. We must learn their success secrets, implement their formula into the underperforming classrooms, and turn our public school system around. The sooner our youth realize that they are worth it and want them to become successful, our nation will become better. So, again, let us take a close look at what is working within the private and religious academic arenas and transplants. We learn into the public halls to get the ball rolling in a positive direction. Now imagine an educational system in which all areas are on or nearly on the level playing ground. It sure would take some effort and growing pains; however, the result will be phenomenal!

YOUTH: Youth Then and Now

Have you given much thought to the differences between today's youth and, say, maybe 20 years ago? Let us talk about this subject, and perhaps we can find some similarities and differences. Then, build on the good and eliminate what we see as a setback or a hindrance to progress.

Let us start by realizing the upcoming generation has almost zero imagination. Everything is already imagined for our youth, and casual interactions with humans are becoming fewer and fewer. Not to mention a society of adults that are scared of letting their kids simply be kids. Combine the two, and you have a recipe for disaster. I know I have been guilty of being an overprotective dad for a time or two. But are we providing a disservice to our kids by safeguarding them. Of Course, we are as hard as it is to back away and let them make mistakes of their own; we must act as a society for our kids to grow and progress both as individuals and the collective.

When I was growing up, I was going outside as often as I could. It was football, baseball, tag, hide and seek, and any other games we could play. Yes, the occasional fight would break out, but that's normal behavior, right? This experience provided plenty of lessons, and more importantly, how to and how not to interact with others. Today's youth is missing out on that critical piece of the puzzle in human development—lack of ability to effectively communicate causes some significant problems and a host of issues. I find myself in the same situation with my kids. I have to remind myself quite often to make them put down the electronics and spend some time interacting outside with others, including playing games with each other or with my wife.

Getting away from all the technology and getting involved with others is necessary for a well-rounded human. It also develops a little tuff skin, some grit if you will. Playing an organized sport is a lifesaver for plenty of kids, particularly the kids that come from undesirable areas with parents that do not discipline or have the time to teach the fundamentals because they are holding down multiple jobs. Due to their circumstances, think how many kids miss out on those opportunities to know fault of their own. Some fantastic athletes, maybe future Hall of Famers, possibly some doctors, lawyers, and future educators. All because they were born in the wrong circumstance.

We live in a society where it is more fantastic to go to prison than go to college. The powers that be rather sink money into a "state of the art" prison facility rather than into a dilapidated school system. So how do you think they are placing their bet on our youth? Listen, I think we should put the money to do some good in the education system. Teachers are underpaid, and the schools are falling apart and the textbooks, Lord only knows how out of date they are. Meanwhile, the prisoners need a newer updated life. It makes me sick!

This generation, where every child gets rewarded regardless of performance or lack thereof, leads us down a dangerous path. How can you not want our children to strive for the best and allowing them to accept their mediocre performance as good enough? Mediocrity is a horrible trait for children, and we did it. Did we let them down? Rewarding mediocrity is the first thing we must change. Let us bring back hard work, patience, and personal accountability; also use the saying "practice pays off." Let our kids know that they did not do good enough and that it is okay to try harder. With hard work and practice, you will get better. You see, as they get better, we as a whole get better. We all benefit from our youth working hard and getting better and pushing toward perfection in their craft, whatever that may be.

Is our youth smarter than us? I think in some ways, yes and in some ways no. They certainly have all the information they desire instantaneously to become more intelligent than we ever had. They can also process a lot more information than we could have when we were at that particular age—their exposure to so much information could help and hurt in some cases. The critical thinking aspect is almost completely gone. If you have all the information you want at your fingertips, why do you have to think? Then I suppose you begin to believe everything you read at some point. Does this sound familiar? Well, doesn't it? If you believe everything you read, people can write what they want you to think and create your new reality.

Man, if you look back at the way my generation grew up, more than half of what we did would be considered taboo today, and yet we survived. So, what happened in the last 20 to 30 years? Is it one thing or a bundle of different changes that we made thinking we were doing some good?

The way the world is more open now

has negatively affected the way we are raising our youth, undoubtedly

The way we are protecting, or shall I say not, safeguard our youth. What a grand opportunity we as a nation provided to our enemies to interact with our youth. We are providing the leftist with the chance to feed their radical agenda to our children. Our children's minds are so vulnerable to manipulation with the openness of the web. We must pay close attention to what our youths are engaging in regarding leftist propaganda. A lot changed since my childhood, and the openness combined with the eagerness for control of our kids' minds is breathtaking.

PROTECTING YOUTH

Protecting youth from the youth!

Someone, please help me understand this mindset of America not being nor ever have been great. How is this possible? Please, someone, help me understand, this belief of America not being great is going too far nowadays. Someone needs to put a stop to this. Let us ask why are we Americans great? Why would you stay if you do not like America? The mind of the infantile college-age adults makes me crazed. Where is the loyalty? Where is the love of country? Where have we failed? How have we allowed this to happen to this country? These are the critical questions we must demand the answers ourselves.

I believe these kids are brainwashed; you see, this shows the leftist plan to take us out from within our system. My friends, it simply was too far gone to manipulate the older generation! So, they went after the children instead. They are particularly good at what they do, and they have done some pretty fantastic damage thus far. Just look at the moral conduct of the upcoming generation. Horrific, to say the least. I am afraid we do not halt and reverse Course; this is the end of America as we know it!

I understand progress is necessary, but you must maintain the foundation and build and progress around those fundamental truths. The correct path is to get back to the basic founding principles and facts and teach our youth. The path toward love, hope, prosperity, joy, and pride for family, friends, and nation. Pride in oneself! I will work tirelessly so that my daughters not only have pride in their country, family, friends but, most importantly themselves.

FREEDOM

Freedom is defined as the power or right to act, speak, or think as one wants without hindrance or restraint. Freedom, my friends, is the subject that evokes my passion. It is the most fragile and vital topic to keep relative in your child's life. They must know the ins and outs of this fundamental and crucial human right. Make no mistake; this right is under attack constantly. Our children must be well versed in their rights; if not, the rights will slowly one by one disappear. I have personally witnessed certain rights under attack in my life; sometimes, it is every day.

If we want our children to taste freedom in its purest form, then we must push against all resistance to protect freedom. Thank God, we live in the greatest nation that has ever graced the planet. We certainly are the last stance of freedom and hope, and we must protect that at all costs. There are so many folks abroad but right here at home that would love us to fail as a country and not fulfill our promise as a nation to ourselves. A guarantee to every American that your freedoms will not be infringed upon by anyone. And indeed, not our government. I will do my part to make sure my children know what their rights and freedoms are. It just takes one family at a time to get started. It only takes you to start educating your family! The more ourselves and our children are armed with knowledge, the less likely we are to get robbed of our fundamental freedoms not only as Americans but also as humans.

I would like to explore several of the freedoms and basic fundamental rights bestowed upon us as humans. Amongst these are the building blocks of the greatest nation ever to exist. Freedom of religion, speech, assembly, and the right to bear arms, to name a few God-given rights. Most of these, if not all, God-given rights are under attack.

Let us look at the hottest topic of the times, which is the right to bear arms. Now I understand that it was to protect a citizenry from a tyrannical government when it was written, and I agree wholeheartedly with this and certainly understand the why. To expand on this, I also believe that you have the right to protect yourself and your family property included. It is my opinion that if you think otherwise, you are delusional. I cannot understand the mindset that limited weapons equals limited crime. It sounds infantile, but the criminals who commit violent crimes do not care about the law, particularly a law limiting weaponry.

I will not waver in my view to my right to protect myself, family and make sure my children are well aware of their right to bear arms and defend themselves. They are pretty young now, but I look forward to the day when as a family, we can start to build a relationship safely and responsibly with a weapon. This way, they can be responsible gun owners but also exercise their right to protect themselves.

To preserve our republic, I will do my part to pass this fundamental right to my children before the right becomes limited or diminished in any way. I suggested if you feel as I do, you should do the same. You and your family should train responsibly. The right to bear arms is entirely under attack, and it is being done very deliberately by our government. The fact that we take arms is genuinely the last stand against a tyrannical government. Although I do not believe that this will ever happen, I think we must stay vigilant and abreast of any changes in the attempt to remove guns.

How about the Bill of Rights amendment #1 freedom of religion, speech, and press? What a fantastic right. The precious right to worship whomever and whenever you want. People all over the world are

Persecuted and even killed for their religious belief. The right to free speech is fantastic; even though you may disagree with the person with opposing views, it is their right to express it. Their opinions also need protection because if you allow anyone to become silenced, you will lose what makes America the beacon of freedom. It has always been and continues to be this very day.

I love the freedom to my very core; I believe that every person is created equal, and citizen's God-given rights should not be infringed. My children may have opposing views than myself, and I will encourage their expression of those views without indoctrination. That is what freedom is all about your choice. Your beliefs to live your life as long as your beliefs harm no one, then, by all means, indulge. Many parents on either end of the spectrum indoctrinate their children before getting a chance to formulate their own opinions. Give our children the facts and the truth and allow them to develop their own opinions. Their opinions may not be the same as ours, but alas, it is honest, and it is their own.

The precious gift of freedom is unique and needs preserving to pass on to our kids to enjoy, then preserved and passed on and on.

I will do my part and pass it on to my beautiful girls and make sure that they understand the responsibility that goes along with preserving freedom. I will also make sure they know all their rights; that is their birthright, after all.

I do not understand the youth today concerning their rights and fully understand the consequences of being gone. With all the ignorance indoctrinated in our children concerning the rights, they played right into the hands of the men and women who wish to destroy us. So, I would encourage anyone who is not versed in their rights. To immerse themselves in the literature that defines and separates us from the world and begin to understand what is at stake if our rights were lost.

Unfortunately, freedom is not free, and that upsets some Americans. The leftist view of the defense of liberty in this perspective is a barbaric and uncivilized view we hold. Sorry but this is the way it is; as brutal and insensitive as this may seem at times, this is the truth. Freedom is not free, and it will never be. It is under attack, maybe more so today than at any time in recent history. I am a freedom-loving, God-fearing man, and I plan on raising my girls the same. They have people in some cultures that would love to see me tortured and killed for my beliefs. I can understand people feeling this way abroad, but you find it increasingly that people feel this way here in our nation. Scary!

We must keep our youth on Course and teach them their freedoms and God-given rights. That gives them and us the best chance to prevail against the attack put forth by the leftist in the nation.

PROTECTING FREEDOM

Unfortunately, many people would like to see America lose, some live here, and some live abroad. Although this is difficult for some to understand, we must do whatever it takes to protect ourselves and our way of life, including information gathering by any means necessary, which includes the use of torture. In my opinion, that is okay to keep our nation safe. My opinion is not nor will ever be a popular opinion to hold. However, it is fundamental to the preservation of freedom. I feel sympathetic to those who have a different view, and I would not try to sway their opinions. However, I will like them to open their eyes a little and realize that it is evil globally, and torture sometimes is a necessary means to maintain our freedoms.

War! Now there is a subject that is a hot topic all the time. Some are pro-war, and some are against war. I feel that freedom is not free, and war is unavoidable at times. We must exhaust all other options provided to us first and allow war to be the last option, of Course! This is not always the case, and we find ourselves in a battle at times. I refuse to believe that any soldier died in vain or in any way, not advancing freedom and or freedom around the world.

While raising my children, I will let them know the pros and cons of the good and the ugly of war and allow them to formulate their own opinion. I wish more parents would have the same mindset and deliver honest facts to make their own decisions on various topics. I understand that they will not arrive at the same conclusion, but it will be open and their opinion. My children are taught to respect someone else's opinion, regardless of how different it may be. If we are going to maintain your freedoms, this approach is imperative.

Raising the next generations of great Americans will not come without significant resistance from those with a more liberal viewpoint. We must stay the Course and focus on the future of our nation. I believe we may be two generations away from losing the most generous country ever, which is a government by the people for the people. We can go one of two ways. We can get our CANS back to the basics or continue on the same Course to a socialistic type of governing. It is our choice!

Protecting freedoms is an approach that must come from inside the nation to outside around the world. We must not shy away from the fact that we must often fight to hold on to the brilliance of freedom. Sometimes we may have to fight fire with fire when necessary. We also must arm our children with the knowledge needed to secure freedom and maintain independence. My fear is once freedom is gone, it is gone, never to return. I know many people who do not agree with a lot of my viewpoints, but I believe I am on the right side of the issue and will defend it tirelessly.

Let us take a few pages here and discuss some of the differences between the Left-leaning viewpoint and the Right-leaning viewpoint.

POLITICAL VIEWPOINTS

Political viewpoints are the topic of the hour, indeed. Political correctness! Political correctness is one of the issues most debated in every corner of our country. The problem lately seems less and less politically correct to discuss, which is sad in many ways. We must remove this political correctness for the next generation and allow them to express their views openly and without persecution. It would be a crime to enable them to fall into the same habits we hold concerning political correctness.

I do not understand the left's point of view on a lot of matters. This does not mean I am opposed to their viewpoint. I am pretty sure that they feel the same about me and my viewpoints. The leftist in this country would like to change the very foundation of the nation. I am convinced of this. I feel this in my very core and the extreme leftist are raising their next generation of leftist, so if we do not get the situation under control and arm our children with morals, rights, and most importantly, God, we will lose our nation as we know it. The leftist in this country hates what the United States stands for. I have seen more and more this pure antipathy for the very symbol of freedom, our flag. Our flag is sacred and should be treated as such. The animals in the street burning and stomping on the flag is a disgrace. I am not saying this is a practice by all leftists, but I can confidently say that no one from the right feels the same sentiment concerning the flag.

The punishment should be reinstated when it comes to the desecration of the flag. What is wrong with a fine if you are caught desecrating the flag? If it happens more than once, maybe some jail time will do! I believe it is a spit in the face of those that have given the ultimate sacrifice for freedom, including the families of the fallen. This is what I meant when I said freedom is not free; it costs and costs dearly; this is why I despise people who desecrate the flag; it is the very symbol of freedom. The political viewpoints of the right and left are opposites as it pertains to every crucial political topic. This was not always the case. Before the latest thrust to control our children's political mindset, the left and right were reasonably close on most vital political points. The rapid deterioration in conservative thought in our children has truly spotlighted the urgency to get back to Americanism and the values that made America great. The leftist viewpoint is nothing more than socialism through thought control. And by the looks of things, the left has been successful.

I eagerly await the day when conservatives can take front stage, and our Cans can get back to the right's viewpoint: bringing morals, exceptionalism, and pride in one's nation. Moreover, not believing in the left's brainwashing and victims' mentality. After reviewing both viewpoints about politics, it is abundantly clear that the Lord is on the right side!

BORDER

Borders is one of the hot topics, especially in the recent presidential election we just had. It seems that those on the right would love to have a healthier, more secure border on our southern border. I believe it would most certainly benefit us as a nation to provide a robust southern border. The arguments against a strong barrier are feeble. How can we not have a strong border? How can the protection of the men and women of this nation not be the top priority? It seems that either some men and women believe they can benefit somehow by allowing people to immigrate to our country illegally, or they would like to see the face of America begin to change. It is not that men and women on the right are opposed to immigration. We are opposed to illegal immigration; there is a big difference!

The men and women who are fleeing them

nation for a better life is coming here and benefiting from a system designed for them to prosper. The big problem is that they come here legally at a temporary status and overstay their legal status and become illegal. There is that type of illegal, and there are just come over the border illegally. I am not saying they are not good people mixed in but, it is too easy for someone who wants to do us harm to gain access to the nation. There are plenty of people who wish to do us harm, and they have been people trying to harm us since the conception of our country.

That is why I say if you think we should not have a strong border or do not believe in a barrier at all, you are playing with fire and allowing a flood of potential terrorists in our nation. How do you explain to a loved one someone who was raped and murdered by an illegal immigrant because your belief allowed them to be here in America? This is what liberals fail to understand we are a sovereign nation; we are a nation of laws. There is a correct way to do things and a wrong way to do something. Correctness should not be up for debate. We should have strong borders. End of story! I would agree with a better and faster way to vet the immigrants. Now, that is the correct argument, in my opinion.

I would love for Cans' next generation to grow up in a safe and secure nation like the one I remember. My children and yours deserve the best we have to offer. I am not suggesting we close ourselves off to the rest of the world but merely take a more innovative and safer approach to allow anyone and everyone who desires to experience the opportunity of freedom. My children will understand the importance of borders and border security as they reach the appropriate age, of course. At the ages of 5 and 7, I hardly think it is reasonable to discuss border security complexities. Although it may not make a lousy bedtime story, no doubt it will keep their interest.

If we can teach our youth the importance of a strong border and the complexities of the legal immigration system, the longer this nation will survive. Once proper border control is understood, we as a nation will not just survive but will thrive as our great country should.

PRO-LIFE

I want to move into a very personal subject, which is very much a hot topic to debate. Pro-life echoing the issue of abortion as it relates to and against this subject. Again, I believe that most of the leftists of this country think it is okay to have an abortion. I find this thought quite revolting. I can speak on this subject because I have some experience in this arena, which I will explain later. Abortion is a part of our culture that is wrong. Wrong in a lot of ways. We are, in a sense telling our youth that it is okay to be irresponsible, have sex, get pregnant, and then have an abortion and all is okay. If we are not judged here, my friends will undoubtedly be judged in the afterlife. This should cause some concern for most Americans.

Needless to say, but if you believe in God, then you know that abortion is a sin. History will not be kind to us regarding abortion and how we dealt with this matter. I try to put myself in the shoes of a society that will be much more advanced and not doubtingly smarter than us.

Imagine 200 years from now what would they think of us when we kill babies by the 100 of thousands a year. They undoubtedly will view us as savages, a brutal and purely selfish race, and I believe they will be ashamed of us and what and how we did things as their predecessors on this earth.

What is wrong with no sex until your married? Saving yourself for the right man or woman seems farfetched these days. I guess I am dreaming. I suppose those days are gone. So, let us approach this with an open mind and in a mature manner. We must teach our children responsibility, especially when it comes to their bodies. We must not depend on anyone else to educate our children in the most sacred and intimate parts of our lives. A wrong move was allowing our schools to have the responsibility of educating our children about their sexuality. Not to mention the education they are getting from their friends. I hope I do not fail as a parent raising two daughters when it comes to this subject. Consequences could become life-altering for them, including myself and my wife.

I recently overheard a conversation where one person in the conversation asked the other person what time during the pregnancy it would not be okay to have the abortion? I believe that at no point is it alright. The person went on to answer it is the women's choice, no one else. Okay, so at one month before delivery? Again, women's choice, the man replied. Okay, one week before birth? Furthermore, it is the women's choice. Okay, one day? Yep, the man answered. So, is post-natal okay? Again women's choice, okay, the man answered. I was stunned when I heard this answer. Post-natal abortion is what I am talking about! What a warped mindset; how can we allow this? Post-natal abortion is pure evil as far as I am concerned.

Not saying all leftists share this warped view of pro-abortion rights, but some do, which is scary enough.

As I mentioned earlier in the subject, abortion is a particularly personal subject because I know close acquaintances who have experienced the pain and guilt associated with the tragedy of abortion. The shame associated with abortion is a long-lasting disaster and should never be an option. We must show our children the right way of handling their sexuality and desires. And lead them down the righteous path, whereas we have failed for generations.

May God bless our children born and unborn.

LGBTQ RIGHTS

Let us take a look at LGBTQ rights and the view each side has on this very taboo subject. In many ways, we as humans have come far concerning LGBTQ rights, but some believe we have plenty of roads still to travel. Some on the right will tell you that homosexuality is a sin. The same folks that believe homosexuality is a sin also believe in God and God's teachings. So, they should know that as a Christian, you should never judge another person. Right! With this, I would say that I am a God-fearing man, and understanding this; I would try never to pass judgment on another person. I consider all people, my brothers, and sisters regardless of their sexual orientation, race, or religious beliefs.

I will gladly teach my children that all men and women are their brothers and sisters. It is not our right to judge. Is homosexuality a sin? This question has plagued us as a race forever. The far-right would like to see gay marriage nonexistent, and the far left would like to see gay marriage pushed upon us. I believe no one should force another person to participate in something against their beliefs. Gay marriage is a subject that should be according to the states, and after all, having this choice is what makes us unique as a nation.

I have great friends and even family members part of the LGBTQ community, both male and female, who love each other very much. Both couples are fantastic people; it is hard for me to believe that they will go to hell or be punished somehow because of who they love. I do know that this view is not extremely popular because I consider myself conservative, and most conservatives will disagree with me. But what I am getting at here is that we should not define ourselves by political parties and conform to their ideals. We should instead find the middle ground and teach the next generation of Cans to be a more free-thinking generation. Compassion, love, and intellect should propel us forward into the next generation and allow America to fulfill its promise to all people. As a country, we have done some marvelous things, but we still have a long way to go in the pursuit of perfection.

I always like to consider what God wants us to do and how God wants us to react or lack reaction. He who is without sin may cast the first stone says it all to me. We must first take care of our own home before we attempt to persecute another. So, please spare me that homosexuality is a sin routine.

There are far worse sins that we all commit daily, including me. It truly irritates me when we cannot in these modern times grasp the concept that we are all God's children, and we must love and accept one another and understand one another. I know I am judged for my lifestyle choices, and I know I am not perfect, so I will not judge another. I refuse to conform to societal norms and persecute someone because of whom he or she loves.

STATES RIGHTS

I believe that the federal government should be extremely limited in its powers. The government should be somewhat of an overseer. The States should retain the right to run their State as they deem necessary. Not allowing the federal government to have complete control over the States was one of the building blocks of this nation, and it is crucial to the future of our country. A government that is over-inflated as the one we have now is dangerous. The government we have now is a nightmare scenario for our founding fathers. So, we must begin the process of limiting our federal government. Arming ourselves with information on how our nation is designed, particularly concerning states' rights, is our first and most crucial step.

States rights are one of the greatest freedoms our founding fathers gave us to create the life we desire. States' rights at their core allow each state to decide how the state will be run. This will enable us to determine what state best resonates with our views, allowing us to determine where we best fit in the united states.

It becomes a problem when the federal government becomes very intrusive in states' rights, and all States, instead of being individual, become more of a representative of the federal government.

The leftist of this nation believes that the federal government holds the answer to all of our problems and should correct such issues. Some leftists believe socialism is the way we should go, and capitalism should be frowned upon as an ideal of the past. A socialistic view will ultimately become a factor in undermining this nation's values put forth by our founding fathers.

Just imagine if the leftist had their way. Imagine a society where the federal government dictated every aspect of life under the pretense that they know better than you. If you remove the state's rights, you will eventually end up with the federal government running everything. It would be just a matter of time before the government would take over all aspects of our lives. We must not allow complete government control to happen at all costs, and I believe they are close, awfully close to achieving the atmosphere they deem appropriate for you and me. The conservatives must start with the youth and try to combat all the negative that transpires regarding the removal of the nation's fundamental essence.

I hope we can get ourselves together as a nation and save this fundamental right. States' rights are at the core of our rudimentary system. States' rights are essential to the growth of our country and must be protected. States' rights are one of the last strongholds we have against the federal government taking control over all of our lives.

Over the last ten years or so, I have

witnessed the federal government taking more and more control over our rights and practically our lives. It has been discouraging, to say the least, watching the government stick its nose in areas such as healthcare. Controlling one's health by the government is a terrifying scenario. The government in healthcare certainly is not needed in this country, not now or not ever.

WELFARE

The view of this subject through the eyes of the right and left of this country should be impressive. Again, this is only my opinion and my viewpoint on welfare. It is also the stance I believe to be essential to educate our children about raising the next generation of Cans. Leftists in this country love to use this to buy votes, essentially putting our country's wellbeing secondary to their desire to win elections. They promise to maintain the handouts with the assumption of you voting for them in the polls. Then claim the right would love to eradicate the handouts. There most certainly needs to be reform but eliminating it will spin our society out of control.

Some on the right have proposed that there should be drug tests on those receiving certain welfare benefits. Why not? It is only fair that if taxpayers have to supply you with certain services to living, you at least should be drug-free. Should you not? Some on the right propose that a possible trade-off with labor or a trade school (earn your keep) get you back out into the workforce. Again, why not? If we are going to pay for your benefit, there should be a benefit for us taxpayers. There are plenty of jobs that need working around the city streets all over the country. We have littered streets and streets that require repair, as well as abandoned properties that require repair. Your pay should be in direct proportion to the service that you provide. For instance, you can make more or less with the job you perform and the amount of time you put into that job.

No one will argue the fact that we have men and women who need help, and it is legitimate, but the truth be told, we have a real generational issue of men and women who will live off this nation and the taxpayers with little to no remorse. The welfare state is killing our society slowly. We must start to wean the welfare generation off of this downward spiral and begin to teach our youth the proper way of contribution and the way of community responsibility.

We need to start now! Raising this next generation of Cans teaches them that we cannot maintain or sustain this way of life. We must show the youth and teach them the proper way to earn a living, and there is more to life than depending on someone else to define your life. The left-most certainly use this technique as a way to maintain control of a voting base. The poor men and women of this nation depend on handouts and do not realize that or simply do not care. Now, we are at a point where this mindset is becoming generational, and it is a "big" issue now. This means that we have allowed an entire generation to learn how to manipulate the system and not need or want anything better for themselves. I see Danger Ahead!

The right-leaning thinking in this country is trying to develop some sort of solution and not just standing by and watching the system cave. The answers give me some hope that we can effectively get this turned around at some point. Allowing people to have a sense of value and worth at the end of the day when they receive that check will benefit them, allowing them to do nothing. It will teach people skills that they have not had the opportunity to learn and that they need to become successful and productive in life.

Can you imagine a nation where most of the citizens of that nation contributed and did not ask for anything in return? But, on the other hand, can you imagine a country where most citizens loved and appreciated that nation and want to contribute instead of taking?

and take. Amazingly enough, we have a citizenry that would rather take instead of contributing. We are the most giving populous in the world to our own, but we also provide aid worldwide. Yet, some in our nation find us and our views on the right repugnant. How can this be?

Arming our Cans with the knowledge that welfare is needed must be monitored closely and controlled not to make the same mistakes as we have and is imperative to our nation's future.

We owe it to ourselves and our youth to begin the long and painful process of fixing this destructive mode we have created.

BORDER CONTROL

The subject of border control should flow from the last topic of welfare in terms that the leftist in this country believe that the men and women who enter the United States illegally should receive certain benefits. Again, keyword illegal how in the world can we allow someone to break into our country and then reward them with services. It is not noticeably clear to me. The men and women on the right are not against those who want to enjoy their freedoms. We would just prefer them to go about it the legal way. I understand that the process needs some reforming, but the traditional way is to allow entry into our nation. This argument is baffling to me. One group would like to have a minimal or no border, and on the other side of the coin, they want a wall on our southern border. I do not know if we necessarily need a wall, but we need something more efficient than what we have.

So, if a wall on the southern border protects the united states' legal citizens, then so be it. We must defend our citizenry before we worry about men and women coming in illegally. Those on the left would love to have open borders giving illegal immigrants access to aids and benefits in exchange for their vote in upcoming elections. If this is allowed in our country, the country as we know it will most certainly be over. So basically, these same people would sacrifice their land for power! It is sick, and it is sad. Unfortunately, this seems to be where we are at as a nation.

What is wrong with borders? What is wrong with enforcing those borders? We know some people want to harm us as a nation. Do you not lock the door to your home at night? To your car? It makes absolutely zero sense to have no border control. It is necessary to maintain your nation's identity. We must make sure our youth understands that we must have borders and protect those borders. We can be a nation that accepts all immigrants, but they must enter the traditional way. Our youth must recognize our enemies and understand the threat they pose to **us.**

Suppose our youth is armed with the knowledge of whom, what, and where our enemies are, then they can make an informed decision on who to allow in our nation. Would you not agree? We have failed our youth already and allowed millions of illegal immigrants to come and stay. It is not very fair to those who wait years to get here or to our youth who will eventually enter this competitive job market. Our next generation of Cans are robbed of opportunities and benefits that are theirs, and it is their birthright, no one else's.

It is ridiculous to allow this to continue. Giving away our children inheritance should go

When they begin to mature and understand what has taken place, the youths are openly robbed, which is undoubtedly taking place all over this nation. If allowed to continue, we will indeed lose the promise of this nation. My view may come across as harsh, but if we continue to enable 3rd world people into the country, our nation will undoubtedly reflect the collective. No? This creates a significant issue where America the great becomes America, the 3rd world nation. Please do not be naive to believe that it will not happen. By all means, it can and will happen if you do not stop this madness and close the borders.

THE SECOND AMENDMENT

This debate has been going on for quite some time, and I do not think the left and the right will find much common ground on this topic. As it sits now, the leftist would like to see the process of getting weapons more difficult, if not an impossibility. At the same time, the right-leaning in this nation sees it as a citizen's right to purchase a gun to defend yourself and your property. The leftist in this country believes that if you remove the nation's guns, the crime will go down or be emptied altogether. I think that to be true to some extent. I tend to believe that you may see gun violence go down, but I also believe you will see a rise in knife violence.

I believe it is logical to think that

we will not eliminate violence by removing or restricting the ability to acquire a weapon. The simple fact is that the gun did not harm or kill anyone. It was the person handling or rather mishandling the firearm that caused the damage. Therefore, I do not see how you can blame the weapon for killing people or peoples. That type of thinking is crazy, in my opinion.

Also, thinking about the founding fathers' thoughts on the second amendment, I believe it is necessary to have an armed citizenry to protect against a tyrannical government. They had first-hand knowledge of an authoritarian government and how they could ruin the united states, so they wisely added the second amendment so this may never happen to us as a nation. The fantastic thing is, if you think an authoritarian government is a possibility, you are considering a lunatic of some sort. Sorry, but I think the government becoming tyrannical is not a farfetched possibility. We have and have had many examples of authoritarian governments throughout history, and I would rather stay protected than be caught unprotected.

I will do my part to raise Cans' next generation to understand the importance and history behind owning a weapon. I will also personally teach my children the correct and incorrect ways to handle a firearm. I want them to be highly comfortable handling a gun and the importance of not abusing this precious right. The more of the next generation we can provide such a disciplined education for weaponry, the better off we will be. However, if we do not educate our youth on this subject as a nation, my fears may come to fruition. The concerns of the leftist in this country removing guns is a real fear for me. The leftist in this country will not hesitate for one second when the guns are removed to push their agenda, which is to take down America and all that we as Americans stand for.

But with that said, I do not believe the government removing the guns will be an easy task. It will come with quite a cost, a revolution, no doubt. Some will hand them over, but some certainly will not.

All it will take is the first shot, the first shot of a citizen protecting their property and right. This one-shot will send this country back into a revolution. Think about the loss of life! To me, it is not worth the risk, but to some, mainly on the left, it may be worth the risk. As a country, we have seen enough bloodshed over the last several hundred years, and we certainly do not need it anymore, especially our citizens. Again, this may seem a bit far-fetched from the thought of another revolution. In all reality, we are one gunshot away! Concerning the disarming of the populace of this nation.

GOD and COUNTRY

This country was founded on Christian values and must remain this way at all costs. We have grown accustomed to allowing the minority in this country to dictate what the majority must do. Allowing the minority to dictate is a load of crap if you ask me. We care more about political correctness in this country than we do about doing the moral or right thing. This must change! It is changing the core of what we are as a nation and what we stand for.

Our founding fathers made sure God was number one and that God and God's will inspire the principles that make us great. What is wrong with a prayer and a pledge in the morning at school? The fact that is removing the national anthem or the Pledge of

Allegiance from our school honestly scares me. This is a threat to our very core, and we should fight at every level of our government. It makes me sick to think we will cater to the "few" at the expense of the "many," and we do this as a nation far too often. This needs to stop!

The removal of God from the country is a scary reality and a reality that we must exercise extreme caution not to take place. The sad part is that I do not know if, as a nation, we would even care if we remove God from the beliefs of our country. This nation's youth are so preoccupied with social media and video games that they do not even realize that the founding father's promise to them is being stolen. They are allowing the leftists to change the beliefs of the nation. Morally and fundamentally, they are changing our country at its core. Once we allow the leftist to rob us of the promise, we will lose the very foundation of what we are as a nation. This should be and is unacceptable!

Our founding fathers knew without God intertwined in our nation's belief system, we as a nation will never hold up and last the test of time. We have repeatedly tried our short history, and because of our divine promise, we have successfully made it through. Our enemies must realize that God is on our side! We put God first! Like God, we will defend all that is good and just around the world. Because God and God's goodwill is placed first in this nation, we will be and have propelled to the forefront of the world. We are the example and leaders of the free world, and that is because we believe in God.

There cannot be an America without God; America's very foundation is based on the morals and principles that God has laid out. We believe that all men and women are created equally by our creator and that our creator has endowed us with certain rights that all men and women are free. God has brought this country forth through the brilliance of the founding fathers and we will not remove God from God's divine plan. As a country, we have made disgusting mistakes, but, indeed, we have learned from these wrongs and will not and must not go backward.

I will most certainly do my part as a parent raising my Cans in providing them with the truth about our founding and the relationship with God, and the formation of our nation. The fact of our nation's founding must become the center of our country's existence once again and propel us into the future. As I stated earlier, you must watch closely what your children are learning in schools. In my case, I can send my kids to a catholic school, but I still must pay close attention to what is taught. If your children are in a public school, you must; I repeat, you must pay close attention to what our children are being taught. The leftist is clever, and they know if they can get to our children before they see the truth, they can quickly push their agenda without interruption.

First, you must have or find your belief in God, to believe in God's morals and message concerning this great nation! I think that America was not an accident and that God graces us, and we are the example for the rest of humanity on how to have a free nation. A road map, if you will, to bring God and the world together. Now, imagine the teachings of God adopted by the rest of the world. How amazing would this world be if God's love ruled? Now mix in some common sense, and you have a world we all could be proud of as Americans. First, we must begin at home and be the teachers and leaders of our families. I understand that God is almost a taboo subject now, and Christian values have increasingly become more and more unpopular, but we can, and we must make God first! If we make God first, sit back and watch the transition for the better both individually and nationally. It will be remarkable! I believe if you bring God to the very Front of this nation, you get the country further and further away from demise. We soar with God or perish.

FREEDOM: GOD'S GIFT

The greatest gift God has bestowed on humanity is freedom. Freedom to choose what we want regardless of what others want for us or think. The thought of not having freedom is terrifying. The truth is, as time goes on, this nation allows the government to take more and more of our freedoms away. We are falling into the leftists' plan, and they want to take as many of our freedoms as possible. The leftist would love to take control of our daily life. The leftists believe that they know what you need better than what you do. Leftists will be more than glad to direct you and to control you if you just let them.

Freedom is the fundamental basis of our country. Simply, without freedom, there will be no America! I thank God that I was on this earth while America is in existence. If you look to history and see how other countries operated, some still do today; it is horrifying. But, as we look back in history, we can begin to see how lucky we are to live in this country. Never has a nation based solely on freedom ever been attempted. It makes me feel pretty special to be a part of this nation and the world's freedom experiment.

You must admit that life is good in America, especially compared to other nations in the world. It breaks my heart to see the younger generation take it for granted and not realize the sacrifices that have been made for this nation and the citizens. Gifts made to pave the way for us not to sacrifice as much as the previous generations. We are fortunate to be here at this time. Yet, time and time again, we find a way to mess it all up. I do not know if it is a lack of knowledge or not understanding the experience that has been provided but, we are allowing us freedoms to become hijacked one at a time. Once removed, it is improbable our freedoms will return.

I could not imagine my life without freedom; I have been free my whole life.

I do not know what it is like not to be free. It drives me crazy when I see these kids not appreciate what we have and then have the audacity to claim oppression. I cannot believe they genuinely feel this way. It is the leftist that has infiltrated the fabric of our educational system and brainwashed our kids. This is why we must start to fight back and not allow the leftists to continue to brainwash our kids. We may be a generation away from losing our nation and the morals and beliefs that make us great. We must teach the next generation of Cans what our freedoms are and why we must protect them. Teaching them the truth seems simple, and it is! Let us teach them the truth. Not a watered-down version of the truth but the ugly, dirty, and violent reality. This way, they can see the deception coming and are armed to deflect the lies and the brainwashing that lies ahead.

Freedom comes at a price, and many young men and women have paid the ultimate price for our nation. May God bless them and their families; without their sacrifice, we would have no freedoms and would be under the control of another government.

We must bind together and fix the severe issues we have in this nation before it is too late. My children, your children, and their children are depending on us to get this right. It is time to take the country back and bring this nation to its promise, and to exemplify the meaning of greatness once again. Our founding fathers had a vision for this nation, and we are way off Course. If we do not halt this decline, we are doomed, in my opinion.

If left up to the leftist in this country, we will all become dependent upon a government that will control every single aspect of our life. It scary when you think about the government controlling every part of your life. That someone you do not even know is making decisions for you and your family. This cannot happen here! We have come too far as a nation to go backward, and it will take radical strategic changes to the areas mentioned above. The time to start is now and is quickly diminishing.

Our plan should bring this nation back to the moral, God-loving, and exceptional country it used to be. Most of us should agree that this government is too intrusive and inflated and must be slowed down. Become more of its promise to us. Become a limited government ran by the people and for the people.

I must admit dealing with this generation is difficult, not all, but a few of them make it difficult. The ones I have the privilege to have dealings with are mostly pathetic and spoiled. They have no morals.

religious code and are just merely weak-minded. This was one of the primary reasons I am writing this book because if this is the example of what our next leaders will become, saving our nation has become urgent. If not now, then it will surely be too late! I feel very strongly about the timing. I am a father of two beautiful daughters, and I must try as hard as possible to leave them with a great nation. A nation better than what I had. Do not get me wrong, the country I have now is excellent, but I want a better country for my daughters.

Let us wake up and find courage, America! Let us take our nation back. We must begin with education. We must support and backup our teachers with whatever they need so they may become successful again. Let us face the fact that they are playing the role of a teacher and play the part of the parents. We must start with our educational system because we are nothing without our youth, particularly an educated youth. When you see and hear the way the youth expresses itself these days, it is very apparent where and how we have failed our youth and in return ourselves.

Where I live, it is very apparent what can happen when you lose the battle of morality. It is scary when 13-year-old kids are killing other 13-year-old kids. The youth have zero respect for life, zero respect for themselves, and zero accountability. They were not born killers. We, as a society, have created them. They have no hope and no other way, and this is all they know. I am not saying we can save all the youth, but we can try. It may be too late for this generation. We must start on the current and the up-and-coming generation.

So, we must start bringing up serious issues and not sweep them under the rug any longer. More importantly, family structure or lack thereof is one of the major problems our country faces. Once we allowed the government to step in and begin to raise our kids, we have lost, and they have won. As we touched on earlier once, they gain access to us children's minds, the government can control what and how much of the information they learn. Let that sink in for a moment. Pretty scary! They can write any history that they want and, in return, dictate the present and future! Amazingly, we have allowed them to buy their way. Speaking! Shame on us as the parenting generation.

SOCIAL MEDIA

There is an extreme risk with social media and the brainwashing of our youth. The amount of time our children spend fixating over and with social media is astronomical. So, it makes sense that the leftist will infiltrate this outlet because of the large number of viewers that can be reached. You have to monitor what is being viewed on social media by your children closely. The leftist has and will use this platform to, in a sense, brainwash our youth.

The great delusion will be disguised in social media. Social media is hazardous and will eventually become the source of most human interactions instead of face-to-face interactions. There are plenty of implications to the humanistic communicative outline derived from a lack of visual communication. Understanding one's full intentions can be lost within social media, much like texting without punctuation. The accurate interpretation is lost.

However, this would be the least of the future problems which can and most likely will occur. The damage afflicted by such a platform can be enormous. The ability to direct and influence the misinformation that our children consume in conjunction with academic indoctrination can be irreversible. Moreover, the ones who control the platform control your opinion and who will digest your ideas, thus limiting your freedom of speech.

Needless to say, these conglomerates have and will continue to use your personal information and online activity to build a profile. A profile that is not used for good but used to determine who will comply with the leftist propaganda and who will reject at all costs moving forward. So this way, it becomes easier to decide who is silenced and who can proceed. However, the likelihood of fighting these companies becoming a reality is slim to none. We must find other conservative outlets to express our views openly without judgment or silencing.

REPAIRING EDUCATION

So, first, I think we waste way too much money on frivolous projects and do not concentrate and fund education as we should. Let us pay our teachers more. I cannot see many objections to that, considering they must play both roles as parents and teachers. Nowadays, even two-parent households cannot be there all the time. Both parents must work full-time jobs to make a living these days. Let us also bring our classrooms up to code new and updated books, even computers and technology. Let us invest, and there is no doubt it will pay off in the long run. When we have a youth entering the workforce that contributes instead of taking from our system, we will become successful again. Allow states to create their environment and curriculum and lets create some competition between the states.

Also, there are plenty of students who want to learn. We must help them by removing the elements that are hindering them. The first but controversial is to remove those students that do not like to know. If you will, the troublemakers allow them to take a GED path; once the distractions are removed, watch how the kids want to learn.

Develop special programs that are fun and educational. Bring back some of the programs that worked, but the budget would not allow for them. Listen to the teachers; they are the ones on the front lines. They are the ones who know what we need to teach our youth to bring them to the next level. Hold the teachers accountable. Teach the children that they are worth it! They deserve the absolute best we have to give. They are our future and must have a great foundation to become successful adults.

I suppose we all know how I feel about education at this point. Still, we cannot hold a conversation about changing our society without getting serious about education, in all honesty. So many of our youth get lost either to the gangs or to the allure of government assistance or both. We know that with government assistance comes government control. We can beat around the bush on this matter, but it is just that. Control! You must vote left because the right wants to take your assistance away. Buying votes, control at its simplest form. Simply let big brother take care of you is the leftist strategy. To me, this generation is too far gone, and we must start fresh with a massive revamping of the educational system.

REPAIRING the YOUTH

We all see the new generation and how they have evolved. The "Millennials" this generation is dubbed. This generation is one of the first generations that came out of the everyone gets a trophy, and no one gets a spanking era. You can see where this mentality has brought us as a nation. Even scarier than is another generation is already making it worse, if not just as bad as the millennials. Not saying all millennials are inept and soft to deal with reality, but a good majority are.

We, as a nation, have done this to the millennials! We have fed them the dream that we all win, and life is easy, and life will cater to your every need. By no fault of their own, they became an ill prepared and entitled generation. We did this! So, now we must fix this. Stop before the next generation grows up and is even worse. Now, in my own house, my wife and I were lucky enough to be raised in an era where there were consequences for our actions, and we had accountability. Therefore, we will raise our children in the same manner. I am not saying that my way is 100 percent effective; however, we must get back to basics based on what we have produced in the latest generation. It is non-negotiable at this point. Get back to the basics and build from there.

Parenting will change; I am not naive enough to not realize that. We tried the entitled approach, and it seems that it has backfired on us. Is it too late to save this generation from itself? In my opinion, yes, now we can save the following generation. Hopefully!

LOOKING TOWARD the FUTURE

There are no limits to this nation's potential to become the greatest nation ever and sustain the time test. Believe me when I tell you, the country is tested to the fullest at this time. Our founding fathers knew that we could become our worst enemies, so they provided us with an outline, a unique path (a diagram) to avoid such disasters. We must take to the design and not try to alter the strategy to suit a few outliers' needs. As we move forward, we must learn from our past and not continue this path of allowing the voice of the minorities to dictate what we should focus on.

Our children need to become a priority in our nation. Let us work together and stop allowing pettiness to ruin this nation. The government has bullied its way into almost every aspect of our lives. No more, we are putting our children and their future at stake for political correctness. It must and will stop!

I still hold an optimistic view of our nation's future and trust in the founding fathers' building blocks. The fathers' instructional road map's divinity will endure in its infinite wisdom and light within the darkness that we are currently facing. The leftist seems to forget conveniently the power and precision of the most remarkable self-governing document written. Moreover, the fathers entrusted the citizen with the building blocks to continue down self-governance and personal achievement and growth.

The path back to forwarding progression lies with and through congressional term limits. Term limits are the only path!

MATURITY

Why is it that generation after generation become belated in their maturity? In my father's generation, it was the norm that a man at eighteen years of age be responsible and self-reliant.

Move out on his own, hold a career, and possibly raise a family if not at eighteen, certainly by the age of twenty; this was the social standard. Now, as I matured and turned eighteen years old, I could not imagine holding down a career or even starting a family. Therefore, these milestones did not happen for me too much later on in life. However, we must consider the fact that I am a procrastinator. Nonetheless, there seems to be a substantial delay in maturity between each generation. This could and will lead to severe consequences in the future!

Understanding the psyche of youth is better left to the experts. However, if I can detect a problem, it must be undeniable. Now with this said, why aren't we trying to correct the issue? One could pose the question that maybe life expectance plays a role in slowed maturity. Meaning the longer we exist on this planet, the slower the maturity rate will become.

As a parent of two young girls, I hold the job to help mold them into responsible, mature adults. My wife and I will not allow society to dictate when my girls will mature or to influence the molding of their maturity. Imagine the advantage they would receive, arriving at maturity a decade earlier than the majority of their peers.

As parents of the future generation of this nation, we must have the youth gain as much time as a mature thinker as possible. As we look at some of the countries around the world, some youth are maturing at an earlier rate than our nations youth. The other nations' head start allows our country to fall behind, and this is unacceptable. We must focus on this issue and develop intelligent solutions to bring our youth to maturity as quickly as possible and remain competitive as possible in the world.

COMMUNISM, SOCIALISM, and CAPITALISM

It is unfortunate that we, as a nation, are heading toward a communistic-style society. I need my children to understand the dangers of this failed societal premise. Some would beg to differ, but in my opinion, it has failed time and time again. Communism is possibly the most dangerous outcome for the next generation of CANS to face.

Unfortunately, we have done nothing to stop a communistic reality from happening.

If molded correctly and the proper programs implemented, we can avoid this disastrous outcome from ever happening. Everything we have worked for as individuals and as a society is at stake. The government is taking control over more and more of our everyday life and this is not for no reason at all. The government always has a plan. Not to benefit society but to help the government. They have already become too bloated and powerful. Therefore, we must pay close attention to government action and not allow the government to take any further steps toward communism.

Again, we must arm the next generation of CANS and not allow this to take place. A communistic or socialistic approach will destroy our nation. This approach must not happen! Instead, we must allow our nation's promise to become fulfilled—a promise of individual freedom in which our founding fathers envisioned many years ago.

The ultimate goal for plenty of leftists, and indeed the vision of a future the current maturing generation would love to see, is socialism. Socialized healthcare and welfare are among the victories the leftist has witnessed in becoming a socialistic nation lately. I understand socialism is an overly complicated subject to dissect, but it seems extremely dangerous to head down this path. Do you want a government to control your healthcare? The governments' intrusiveness has ruined plenty of aspects of daily life. The government has destroyed social security, so what makes you think they can take care of your health. I certainly do not want the government making decisions about my and my family's healthcare.

How fair is it that someone works awfully hard and takes chances that others are not willing to do and becomes successful and gets punished? Not very fair! These actions will undoubtedly diminish hard work and risk-taking. Why should I work hard and take a risk when the government will take my hard work and spread my earnings around to undeserving people? I am all for charity but allow me to pick and choose to whom I want to be charitable. Unfortunately, we are heading in this direction as a nation, and we must halt and redirect ASAP.

Again, I will teach my daughters the Danger of a socialistic nation. We have plenty of examples around the world to review. My daughters must be aware of the dangers and how to combat such a governmental style personally. Socialism has and will fail over and over again.

The best path to prosperity and achievement is capitalism. Rewarding someone for hard work in direct proportion to the goods or service that someone provides is, by all means, the only way to operate a nation. Maybe not the only way but the only way to run a prosperous nation. Those who are unwilling to sacrifice and work hard are generally the ones who complain about a capitalistic country. The leftist in the country is the first to punish those who are considered to be successful. The leftists love to take the money that successful men and women have earned and spread those amounts of money to those men and women considered less fortunate. Possibly to buy votes, one must presume.

Capitalism is the way we must teach our youth. Striving for success is the path I will lead my daughters. My daughters will understand the fundamentals of capitalism and understand why a capitalistic nation is so important to hold on to freedom. In return, I will also teach my children the importance and value of charity.

This way, my daughters can dictate where and when they choose to be charitable with their hard-earned money and not the government using their money to push an agenda, just like communistic and socialistic governments do with their citizens.

SOLUTIONS

I want to take a moment and look at some solutions to correct our youth's path possibly. I see it as minor changes, and solutions are ultimately better than no answers at all. By reading this book, I hope you will start the corrective measures needed to take back our nation and propel us in a more positive direction. So, let us change our FOCUS, do the small changes, and start the shift in a productive direction. We must first, as a nation, realize we have issues. We then can try to understand and get a clear definition of what problems we must fix. Then we can begin the process to correct the path of our nation.

As a nation, it is time to get serious about the serious issues we face. The last generation to reach maturity in this nation is not the best we can offer to the country and the world. So, we must start with our youth and begin to implement morals back into everyday life. Install morals in education and promote morals at home as well. It is my opinion that God is missing in both the home and school. Ever since the leftist have begun removing God from schools, it is my opinion that's when our youth's downfall began. We must bring God back into our classrooms once again. There should not be an argument about God's reinstatement and his teachings because God is all love, and God's instructions are all about love as well.

So, where is it can we find the solutions we need in society today? Well, we can start by learning the teachings of God and emulating his instructions to our children. Then we must get conservatism back into a mainstream way of thinking. Conservatism, in its rudimentary, is the path back to success and accountability. And I look forward to the day we can celebrate conservatism again.

LOSING

This book is just my opinion, and it is not meant to hurt any feelings directly or indirectly. It is simply to get us thinking and possibly develop some positive ideas to get us back on track as a nation. Some of you may feel that we are doing fine as a nation, but I tend to think otherwise.

In writing these words, I thought many of my children and what I can do as a father give them the most incredible opportunity to become successful as an individual and as a part of society. My children and marriage are my most significant accomplishments, and both deserve the same attention and dedication. My children and wife will get a glimpse into my thoughts and understand that we can do our part in raising our two CANS. If we can, hopefully, have some other families get started as well. I am bringing all of us closer and closer to the PROMISE of our nation.

GOD BLESS AMERICA AND THE

NEXT GENERATIONS OF CANS!

www.ingramcontent.com/pod-product-compliance
Lightning Source LLC
Chambersburg PA
CBHW031424210526
45464CB00005B/2036